RAIL ROVER

FREEDOM OF THE SEVERN AND SOLENT

JOHN JACKSON

AMBERLEY

First published 2022

Amberley Publishing
The Hill, Stroud
Gloucestershire, GL5 4EP

www.amberley-books.com

ISBN 978 1 4456 9018 6 (print)
ISBN 978 1 4456 9019 3 (ebook)

British Library Cataloguing in Publication Data.
A catalogue record for this book is available from the British Library.

Typesetting by SJmagic DESIGN SERVICES, India.
Printed in Great Britain.

Contents

Introduction

For as long as I can remember, railway enthusiasts and lovers of train travel have taken advantage of rail rover tickets. To this day, these rover tickets continue to offer a flexible and attractively priced product for enthusiasts of rail travel. They are provided, perhaps reluctantly, by today's railway operators with little or no product promotion.

I remember a fellow rail enthusiast from Cheltenham Spa showing me this particular rail rover ticket. It was around twenty-five years ago and it intrigued me because it was printed in typical 'rail speak'. The ticket read 'FOSS Rover'. The only 'FOSS' that I could recall was the Roman road, Fosse Way, but there was surely no connection?

It was only on further investigation that I identified its full title and was pleasantly surprised at the geographical area it covered. Since then, I have lost count of the number of times I have used these tickets over the last quarter of a century or so in pursuit of my hobby.

The Freedom of the Severn and Solent (FOSS) referred not to a Roman road, but to two of England's most significant rivers. I soon realised that this 'Freedom of Severn and Solent' area of validity included a wide diversity of exciting rail travel opportunities for a keen enthusiast and rail traveller like me.

The ticket's geographical area extends from Cardiff, Newport and Bristol in the west all the way to Swindon and as far south as Portsmouth, Weymouth and Tiverton Parkway. In addition, the ticket coverage included two of my favourite locations, Westbury and Eastleigh. To the north, the ticket also enables travel in the triangle of Worcester, Cheltenham and Gloucester.

The purchaser is offered a choice of variations on the length of the ticket's validity. These options include a ticket valid for any three days' travel across seven consecutive days or travel on any eight days in a given fifteen-day period.

As I live outside this ticket area, the eight days in fifteen option was a particularly attractive offer. I was soon enjoying time away, usually spending four days using the ticket with one week based either in Cardiff or Bristol, and then a second week with a further four days centred on either Eastleigh or Westbury, with a few days at home in between. I recognise that this is one of the benefits of both retirement and qualification for a Senior Railcard.

Such rail rover tickets have long been seen by enthusiasts as a flexible way of travelling around a particular area of the country for a relatively low daily rate, particularly when compared with rail travel using conventional day return ticket options. The privatisation of our railways has only added to the ticket's attraction, as the ticket places little restriction on which railway company's trains can be used within the given ticket area.

This book in no way attempts to list the full terms and conditions that apply to such tickets. Suffice to say that rail rovers are treated as off-peak tickets, generally available for travel after 09.00 Mondays to Fridays and anytime at weekends and on bank holidays. An internet search of 'GB Rail Rovers' will give the reader all the details that he or she may need. As always with ticketing on our rail network, there are some further provisos with some additional workings specified, enabling an earlier weekday start from some stations.

There has been a great deal of change across the whole of the UK rail network since I purchased my very first of these Freedom of Severn and Solent rover tickets. In particular, the privatisation of our railways in the mid-1990s has seen the area's passenger services divided into several private franchises. More recently, the Great Western Main Line (GWML) has seen the completion of electrification, at least on the stretch between Swindon and Cardiff, via Bristol Parkway. As a consequence, the iconic high-speed trains have been displaced on London services.

One of the attractions the ticket offers when using today's privatised railway is its validity across all passenger train operators' services within the region. These services are in the hands of a number of different operators, with First Great Western and South West Trains covering most of the region between them. To the west, Cross Country Trains and Transport for Wales also offer regular service options. The list is completed with both Southern and West Midlands Railway serving stations on the edge of the rover area.

The price of these rail rover tickets rises annually, usually in June, in line with the annual rate of inflation. In summer 2021, the cost of the 'eight in fifteen' day ticket option, when purchased along with a Senior Railcard, was £58.40. This equates to a little over £7 per day assuming use over the full eight days available. This figure rises to just over £14 per day if the 'three in seven' option is chosen.

Here are just two examples of the ticket's offerings. First, the user can travel the whole of First Great Western's Cardiff to Portsmouth Harbour route via Bristol, Bath, Westbury, Salisbury and Southampton. This offers a round trip of over 200 miles. Taking around eight hours, this return journey is easily achievable in daylight through most of the year.

Secondly, the Cross Country Trains journey between Cheltenham Spa and Tiverton Parkway is one of just under 200 miles. On these services a much faster journey time is on offer, with most trains taking around ninety minutes in each direction. In my opinion, both these examples demonstrate just how attractively priced this particular rover ticket is.

Rail privatisation also saw freight services placed in the hands of private operators, with all the main freight companies currently having at least one regular service operating within the ticket's area. It is, however, an area of extremes. For example, the whole of the county of Dorset is currently without any regular freight traffic. By contrast, the stone quarries of the Mendip Hills and the remaining steel works in South Wales offer much to draw today's enthusiasts. In the south-east of the area, there are regular container trains running to and from the docks at Southampton – day and night on weekdays.

In this book we take a look across the whole of the ticket's geographical area and broadly cover the period during which I have been using these tickets, that is to say from 1990 to date. As a footnote, a glance at the map at the front of the photo section will show that the railway junctions of both Didcot Parkway and Exeter fall just outside this ticket's area of validity. Both popular locations have, therefore, been excluded from this publication.

The photos that I have selected on the pages that follow demonstrate many of the region's changes, ranging mainly from the privatisation era of the 1990s through to the present day. Our journey around this extensive area starts at Cardiff in the west and ends at Portsmouth and Weymouth in the south-east and south-west corners. The sequence I have used is outlined in the contents page. Almost all of these photos have been taken either at railway stations within the ticket area or a short walking distance from them. I acknowledge that one of my favourite locations, Fairwood Junction, near Westbury, is an exception, being a brisk walk at around a mile and a half or so from the main station at Westbury.

The Freedom of Severn and Solent ticket covers an area with much to offer the rail enthusiast and leisure traveller. It is still possible to opt to see today's express passenger trains alongside a selection of freight traffic, particularly at railway junctions such as Cardiff and Eastleigh. It's also possible to take a gentler-paced train ride and enjoy some of England's delightful countryside scenes from the train window.

As always, whatever your preference, I hope you enjoy your journey through these pages as much as I have enjoyed compiling them.

John Jackson

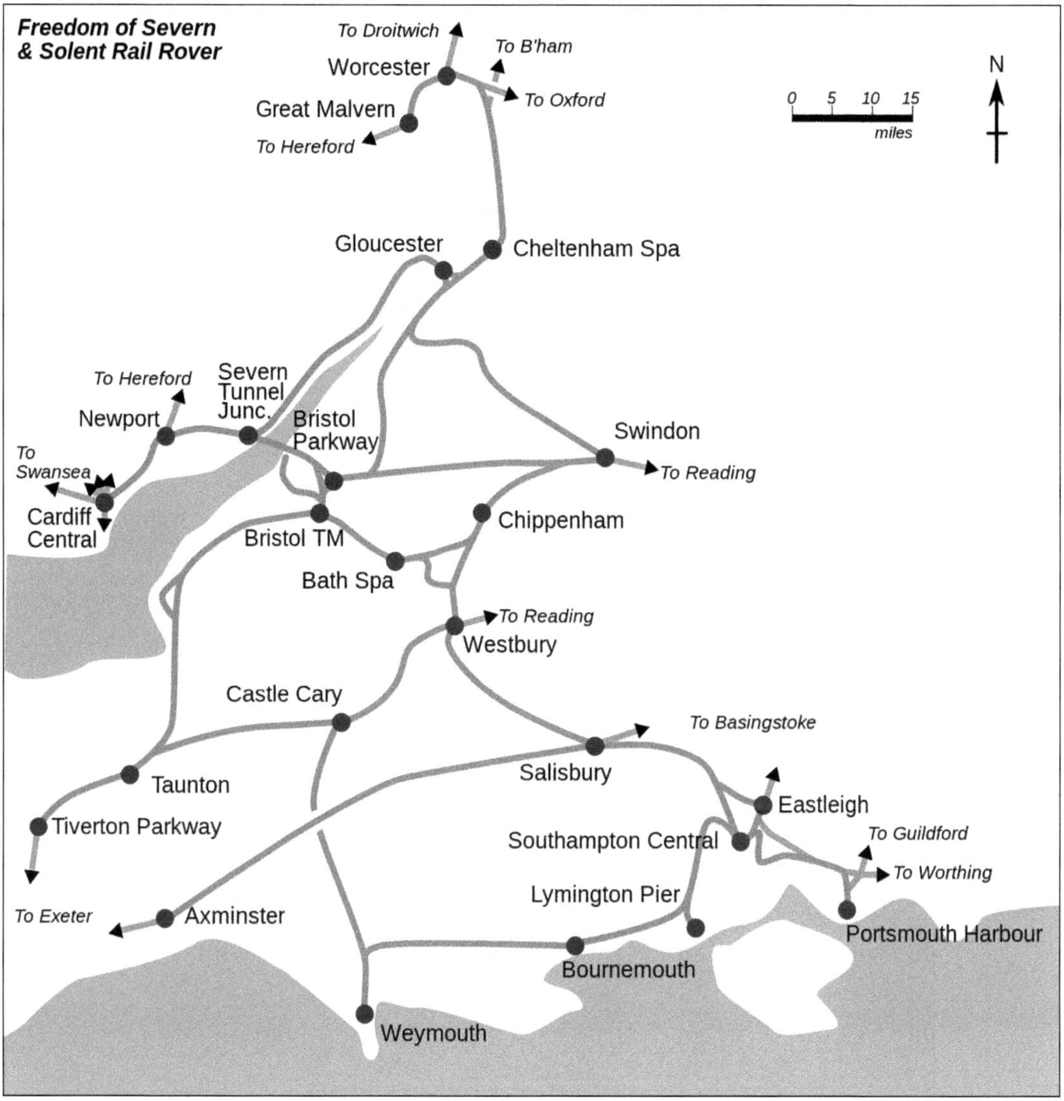

Rail Rover: Freedom of Severn and Solent – area of ticket validity. This rail map shows the area in which the ticket is valid for travel. In fact, the area's boundaries have not changed very much, if at all, for as long as I can remember. A new station in the north of the region, named Worcestershire Parkway, has opened since this map was produced.

Cardiff

We commence our journey around this rail rover area at its most westerly point, Cardiff Central. Most of the Welsh capital's local services are operated by Transport for Wales (TfW). On 5 June 2019, single-coach unit No. 153327 arrives at Central station on a local City Line service to Coryton. TfW took over operation of these services in October 2018. Prior to that date the previous franchise holder, Arriva Trains Wales (ATW), had run these Welsh services for around fifteen years.

The familiar Class 142 'Pacer' units are coming to the end of their working lives, and not before time in the views of many regular users of them. They have been regular performers on South Wales services on the City and Valley Lines throughout the period of ATW holding the franchise. On 16 September 2019, No. 142083 stands at Cardiff Central on a local suburban service from Radyr to Coryton.

These local diesel multiple unit services in South Wales have been supplemented by the peak-time use of hired in locomotive and hauled coaching stock in recent years. On 17 September 2019, No. 37421 is seen arriving at Central station on a morning Valley Lines commuter service from Rhymney consisting of three coaches.

The previous day, sister Class 37 locomotive No. 37418 is seen at Cardiff Central. It had just terminated on 07.42 service from Rhymney and was about to remove the coaching stock to Cardiff Canton depot for servicing and stabling.

Although Cardiff's Central station represents the western limit of this rover ticket, back in the 1990s the depot at Canton, just beyond the ticket limit, was always worth the ten-minute walk. On this particular day in the early 1990s that walk was rewarded with my first sighting of No. 60004 *Lochnagar* stabled on the depot. The Brush loco had just been outshopped from their Loughborough works and newly delivered to the Cardiff area.

On 18 April 1994, sister loco No. 60034 *Carnedd Llewelyn* is stabled in almost the same location. It is seen from the depot's popular footbridge, which was the official walkway to the diesel depot entrance.

On 12 October 1991, Network South East-liveried No. 47707 Holyrood is a less common visitor to the depot. It was particularly surprising to find it here as the author had been hauled by this loco just a few days earlier between London Waterloo and Basingstoke.

Today, the footbridge and that entrance to Cardiff Canton depot are long gone. The area does, however, still see the stabling of both locos and units. On 4 June 2019, No. 67016 has just left Canton sidings and is arriving at Central station to form an early evening departure to Holyhead.

These DB Schenker-owned locos are hired in by Transport for Wales to operate these services. They are serviced at their owners' depot in Crewe, requiring switching of locos between Cardiff and Crewe for maintenance purposes. On 16 September 2019, No. 67012 passes through Central station on one such light engine move back to its Crewe base.

Great Western Railway (GWR), formerly First Great Western, operate hourly passenger services from Cardiff to both Taunton and Portsmouth Harbour. These GWR services are now in the hands of Class 165 and 166 Turbo units, recently displaced following Great Western Main Line electrification in the area around London Paddington. On 17 September 2019, No. 165118 leads a five-car formation on a Portsmouth Harbour service.

Cross Country Trains' passenger services serving Cardiff are predominantly in the hands of their Class 170 units. Proving the exception to the rule, Voyager No. 220032 arrives at Cardiff Central station on 16 July 2015. It will shortly form an early morning service to Manchester Piccadilly, at the time this was the sole working of the day from Cardiff that was booked for a Voyager.

Today, Cardiff sees a steady flow of freight traffic through Central station. These services are chiefly operated by DB Schenker, who have a stranglehold on most of the steel and oil traffic in the area. On 22 February 2018, No. 60054 approaches the station on a rake of loaded oil tanks from the terminal at Robeston, in West Wales, to Westerleigh, near Bristol.

On 4 June 2019, No. 66164 passes in the opposite direction with one of the frequent steel services that DB Schenker operate between the South Wales plants at Llanwern and Margam. It is passing GWR's Hitachi unit, No. 800310, waiting to leave on a London Paddington service.

These freight movements within South Wales necessitate loco positioning moves between the various yards. On 5 June 2019, Nos 66158 and 66019 are seen accelerating away from a signal stop at the west end of Central station on one such light engine move from Newport's yard at Alexandra Dock Junction to Margam.

In South Wales today the coal traffic is much reduced as it is across the whole of the network. Back in 1994, diesel-hauled rakes of 'merry-go-round' coal wagons were the order of the day. On 18 April that year, No. 56073 *Tremorfa Steel Works* heads west through the station on a rake of wagons with canopy hoods, used to prevent the coal blowing while on the move.

Both Freightliner and Colas Rail also handle freight traffic in South Wales. In this view of Cardiff Central on 22 February 2018, Freightliner's No. 66529 approaches from the Vale of Glamorgan lines with a rake of empty flat wagons from Barry. Waiting to head west is Colas Rail's No. 70812 on a working from Westbury to Aberthaw.

Newport

Newport is Wales' third largest city and is situated approximately 12 miles east of Cardiff on the Great Western Main Line. On 1 June 2013, No. 158833 calls on a service to Manchester Piccadilly that will head north up the Marches Line, along the border between England and Wales.

The familiar Arriva Trains Wales (ATW) turquoise colour scheme was carried by all the company's Wales-based units during their lengthy franchise. New operator Transport for Wales (TfW) is in the process of applying its own branding to the fleet. Examples of both liveries are seen at Newport on 16 September 2019 as No. 175002, with TfW branding, passes sister unit No. 175008 (ATW).

The changing traction on services between South Wales and London Paddington is reflected in these two views. On 18 April 1994, high-speed train (HST) power car No. 43005 is seen on the rear of a service about to depart Newport for Paddington. The entire train rake of coaches carries the much-loved InterCity livery.

A quarter of a century later, these London Paddington services are now totally in the hands of GWR's fleet of Hitachi-built replacements. On 16 September 2019, No. 800316 leaves Newport on a service bound for London Paddington.

For lovers of the high-speed trains, there are still opportunities to travel on these iconic machines. They now operate a number of GWR's secondary services, including some Cardiff to Taunton workings. In this view, also taken on 16 September 2019, power car No. 43170 is seen on the rear of a Taunton-bound service. This power car, together with its shorter rake of coaches, all carry the latest GWR livery.

Local trip workings between the various yards in the Newport area meant the small fleet of Class 09 diesel shunters passing through the station were a familiar sight. On 29 April 1999, it is the turn of No. 09203 to pass through on one such working consisting of an assortment of steel wagons. These Class 09 shunters have different gearing than their Class 08 counterparts, enabling a higher maximum speed of just under 30 miles per hour.

Around the time of rail privatisation in the mid-1990s, much of the South Wales freight traffic was in the hands of Class 37 and Class 47 locomotives. On 18 April 1994, No. 37711 passes through Newport station on a rake of short wheel base tank wagons.

On the same day, a Class 47 loco can be seen on the loco stabling point at Godfrey Road in a busy scene that shows two Class 37 light engine moves, with No. 37141 in the foreground. The former stabling point is now part of the station car park.

A few minutes later on the same day and it is the turn of a pair of Class 47 locomotives to head east through the station on a light engine move. The loco nearer the camera is No. 47395, which, having been renumbered back to '47205', has survived and is now preserved at the Northampton & Lamport Railway.

The downturn in rail-hauled coal traffic has been well documented and scenes such as this one are becoming increasingly rare. On 16 July 2015, DB Schenker's No. 66025 passes westbound through Newport with a rake of HTA coal hoppers from nearby East Usk Junction Yard to the coal washery at Onllwyn, near Neath.

The coal traffic may be in decline, but there is still a variety of freight traffic on view through Newport, as these early afternoon workings on 16 September 2019 demonstrate. First, No. 60015 heads west with the loaded oil tanks from Robeston to Westerleigh.

An hour later and Freightliner's Class 66/6 locomotive, No. 66602, heads in the opposite direction with a rake of empty hoppers from Stoke Gifford Yard at Bristol to Port Talbot.

A few minutes later and another Freightliner Class 66 loco, No. 66541, passes through on a container train working from Cardiff Freightliner Terminal at Wentloog to the Suffolk port of Felixstowe.

Finally, the quartet of movements is completed by Colas Rail's No. 70808. It is seen heading west on a rake of cement tank wagons from Westbury to Aberthaw.

Severn Tunnel Junction

As the name implies, the station is situated close to the famous tunnel. It is at the junction of the South Wales Main Line from London and the line from Gloucester to Newport. It is close to the western end of the 4-mile-long tunnel beneath the river estuary. In this station view on 15 September 2019, the electrification of the main lines had just been completed and the section was about to be energised.

On 23 February 2018, HST power car No. 43127 leads a Cardiff Central to London Paddington service eastbound through the station. At the time HST were still operating some services. This particular set carried the earlier livery when the operator was branded 'First Great Western'.

By February 2018, the Hitachi Class 800 units were steadily replacing their HST counterparts. A pair of units, No. 800016 leading No. 800011, have just emerged from the tunnel and are westbound through the station on a Swansea service.

While London services run non-stop through the station, Great Western Railway services between Cardiff and Taunton call here. On 13 November 2017, No. 158798 is seen stopping on a Taunton-bound working. This unit carries a unique livery promoting the local charity Springboard.

The station is also served by Transport for Wales local services between Cheltenham Spa and Cardiff Central, with most trains running beyond there to Maesteg. On 13 November 2017, Pacer unit No. 142010 calls on its journey to Cheltenham as it passes No. 158828 in the adjacent platform, heading in the opposite direction.

Class 150 units are also seen on these TfW services. On 8 November 2017, No. 150285 is seen calling on a service from Cheltenham Spa to Maesteg.

The depot to the west of the station has long gone. The busy junction station does still, however, see a variety of freight traffic passing through. On 8 November 2017, No. 66031 heads west on an empty steel working returning from Round Oak, in the West Midlands, to the yard at Margam.

A few days later, sister DB Schenker loco No. 66007 is seen on another westbound empty steel movement. This train is also bound for Margam on its return from Swindon's Cocklebury Yard.

An hour earlier on 13 November 2017 Freightliner's No. 66952 heads in the opposite direction. The loco is working a container service from Cardiff Wentloog to Southampton.

Direct Rail Services operate just one regular container service that falls within this rail rover area. On 13 November 2017, their Class 66 loco, No. 66433, heads west through Severn Tunnel Junction station on the company's daily working from Daventry's International Rail Freight Terminal to Cardiff Wentloog.

Colas Rail Class 70 locos are regular visitors along the South Wales Main Line. On 21 February 2018, No. 70812 heads east through Severn Tunnel Junction with a rake of coal hoppers from Aberthaw to Avonmouth Docks.

A few minutes earlier on the same day and sister loco, No. 70816, passed through on a less regular working. It was called upon to take the company's track machine, numbered 'DR75407', to the company's servicing depot at Rugby.

Around Worcester and Cheltenham Spa

The Freedom of Severn and Solent rail rover ticket area extends northwards to include both Worcester and Cheltenham Spa. On 7 November 2017, Great Western Railway (GWR) HSTs were still operating London Paddington services from this area. That day power car No. 43094 arrives at Worcester Shrub Hill on a service from London Paddington. Sister power car No. 43133 is on the rear.

For many years, these HSTs operated alongside the small fleet of Class 180 units on these London services. On 15 February 2016, five-car unit No. 180108 arrives at Worcester Shrub Hill station on a London-bound service. The Shrub Hill station area has retained its semaphore signals longer than most.

Worcester is also served by West Midlands Railway units operating local services across the Birmingham area. On 7 November 2017, one of their three-car units, No. 172331 stands in the station's centre road between duties.

Provincial passenger services southwards from Worcester are operated by GWR and serve a diversity of destinations such as Brighton and Weymouth. In 2017, No. 150926, temporarily renumbered from '150126' and formed as a two-car unit, approaches Worcester Shrub Hill station.

The same day, sister unit No. 150233 waits in Shrub Hill station ready to form a southbound service. The unit will take around four hours to complete its journey from Worcester to Weymouth.

In common with much of the UK, Worcester is served by the annual Rail Head Treatment Trains (RHTT) during the autumn leaf fall season. On this afternoon in late November the Colas Rail-operated service arrives at Shrub Hill with No. 66846 leading.

These RHTT trains operate in top and tail formation. Sister Colas Class 66 loco No. 66848 is seen on the rear as the train pauses in the station, with the two railhead treatment wagons sandwiched between the locos.

A far more spectacular Class 66 movement occurred through Worcester Yard, situated to the side of Shrub Hill station, on 15 February 2016. GBRf loco No. 66708 *Jayne* paused here while dragging new locomotive Nos 66777, 66776, 66779, 66778, 66774, 66773 and 66775 on delivery to their new owners, having been unloaded at Newport Docks. No. 66779, in the middle of the convoy, was delivered 'under wraps' and the loco was soon to become a celebrity when it was unveiled in a unique livery and carrying the name *Evening Star*.

The city of Worcester boasts two railway stations. Shrub Hill is the larger, but Foregate Street is more centrally located within the city. Services to and from London Paddington generally serve both stations. On 10 October 2012, No. 180104 has just terminated at Foregate Street on a service from Paddington.

The FOSS rover ticket area extends a few miles south-west of Worcester to the station at Great Malvern. On 15 February 2016, No. 170631 calls there on a service from Hereford to Birmingham New Street.

On 31 May 2012, No. 150107 calls at Great Malvern, heading in the opposite direction. It is leaving on a service from Birmingham through to Hereford.

Cross Country Trains services south of Birmingham take the direct route towards Cheltenham and do not serve Worcester. On 7 November 2017, No. 170522 passes near the site of the closed station at Wadborough on a service from Cardiff Central to Nottingham. This location is just south of the junction where the lines from Birmingham and Worcester meet.

Cross Country Voyagers are the regular traction for their services that cross the FOSS ticket area. Four-car unit No. 220033 heads south past Wadborough on a service to Bristol Temple Meads.

These Cross Country services are supplemented by the company's use of HST sets on a limited number of services from the north of England to Plymouth. In this view, also taken on 7 November 2017, their power car No. 43321 is seen on the rear of a Plymouth-bound service.

The station at Cheltenham Spa is the northern terminus of Transport for Wales services from Maesteg, via Cardiff Central. On 30 May 2012, during Arriva Trains Wales' operation of the franchise, No. 158833 has just terminated and will reverse into the southbound platform for its return to South Wales.

On the same date, First Great Western's No. 150247 is also terminating. This time, the service has arrived at Cheltenham Spa on a local service from Swindon.

Bristol Parkway and Stoke Gifford

Bristol Parkway station opened in 2001 and heralded a new generation of parkway stations. These railway stations generally offer good road transport links. This new station, north of Bristol, provides convenient road access to the M4, M5 and M32 motorways. On 14 July 2015, single-car unit No. 153305 is seen arriving at the station.

The station offers regular services to London Paddington, approximately 110 miles to the east, with all services from South Wales, via the Severn Tunnel, scheduled to call here. On 15 July 2015, HST power car No. 43150 leads a service from Paddington to Cardiff into the westbound platform.

In this view looking west from Bristol Parkway station's overbridge, No. 158953 is seen arriving from the Bristol direction, with the lines to the Severn Tunnel and South Wales veering to the right. The first signs of the forthcoming electrification can be seen in the centre.

On 15 July 2015, No. 158766 waits in the platform at Bristol Parkway to form a GWR local service to Weston-super-Mare, offering the local Bristol traveller a cross-city service.

By the time this view was taken on 22 February 2018 the Class 165 and Class 166 Turbo units had started operation on Bristol-based services. Here, No. 166213 waits to leave on another local service across Bristol.

The station area sees a number of freight movements, chiefly in the hands of Freightliner and DB Schenker. On a wet day in December 2013, Freightliner's No. 66569 heads east through the station on a return container working from Cardiff Wentloog.

The lines to the south side of the station are used for holding freight trains. On 22 January 2014, DB Schenker's No. 66060 is awaiting departure while working a rake of empty hoppers from Wembley through to Moreton on Lugg, on the Welsh border.

Bristol Parkway is situated in the Stoke Gifford area to the north of Bristol city centre. The adjacent yard is home to a Freightliner stabling point. On 21 June 2014, No. 66619 waits in the station platform on a light engine move, which will see the loco cross into the Stoke Gifford Yard.

A perimeter view of the Freightliner stabling point in Stoke Gifford Yard can be achieved following a ten-minute walk from Bristol Parkway station. On 7 July 2013, No. 70013 was among the yard's occupants on view.

A few years later, on 10 May 2019, it is the turn of a more common pair of Freightliner locos to be on view. Their Class 66 loco, No. 66590, is nearer the camera, with sister loco No. 66562 just behind.

Bristol Temple Meads to Tiverton Parkway

Bristol's main railway station is at Temple Meads, well known for its iconic Brunel-designed architecture. On 22 February 2018, Cross Country Voyager No. 220010 stands under the impressive station roof waiting to depart on a service to Manchester Piccadilly.

As already mentioned, high-speed train sets are used to complement the Cross Country fleet of Voyagers. On the same day, power car No. 43366 waits to leave on a service from Plymouth to Leeds.

The local Bristol branch line to Avonmouth and Severn Beach is one of the area's survivors from the days of the Beeching Report and the resultant line closures of many branches. On 18 November 2015, single-coach unit No. 153329 has just terminated at Temple Meads on a GWR service arriving from Severn Beach.

GWR's longer-distance services require reversal at Bristol Temple Meads. On 22 February 2018, No. 158953 is seen arriving on a service from Great Malvern. After reversal, its ultimate destination will be Brighton.

GWR Turbo units are now regular performers on local services in the Bristol area. Unit No. 166208 is seen leaving on a Westbury-bound service – also on 22 February 2018.

GWR's use of HST power cars, working with short, set coach formations, continues on the company's secondary services. On 6 June 2019, No. 43029 leads a rake of FGW-liveried stock into Temple Meads on a Cardiff Central to Taunton service. Sister power car No. 43189 is seen on the rear sporting the revised Great Western Railway livery.

South Western Railway, formerly South West Trains, operate a limited number of through services between Bristol and London. On 22 February 2018, No. 158880 waits to leave Temple Meads on a service to London Waterloo, which will reach the capital via Westbury and Salisbury.

Network Rail test trains are often stabled in the Temple Meads station area in between their duties. On 21 October 2011, No. 31106 was in charge of one of these Network Rail workings from Derby. This veteran machine first entered service back in March 1959.

Temple Meads station sees only a limited amount of passing freight traffic. On 6 June 2019, however, two freight workings passed through the station within the space of forty minutes. First, No. 66572 passed through the platform on a Freightliner container service from the Port of Felixstowe to the nearby freight terminal in Bristol.

Forty minutes later, Colas Rail's No. 70807 heads in the opposite direction working the return cement empties from Moorswater, on the Looe branch in Cornwall, to Aberthaw in South Wales.

Bristol was an important hub for postal movements when the Royal Mail was an extensive user of the rail network. On 18 April 1994, No. 47626 is seen on a short rake of mail vans bound for the north of England later in the day.

Today's visitor to Temple Meads would find it hard to believe this scene from thirty years ago. The extensive Bristol Bath Road depot area was situated adjacent to the station platforms. On 20 October 1990, the depot area contained Nos 47456 and 56051 among this array of locos and units. Today, there are no obvious signs of the depot's existence.

In common with much of the UK, the diesel fuel used by locos at Bath Road depot was delivered there by rail. On 18 April 1994, No. 37798 is in charge of shunting a short rake of these wagons within the depot area.

Just to the east of Temple Meads station is the Traction Maintenance Depot at Barton Hill. There is usually a diesel shunter resident here. On 22 February 2018, No. 08516 was stabled, viewed here from a passing GWR service.

This Barton Hill depot is visited by a variety of locos and units for servicing and maintenance purposes. On 16 July 2015, however, the depot area was home to a railway celebrity in the form of steam locomotive No. 60163 *Tornado*. Again, this view was taken from a passing GWR service.

Great Western Railway has its own depot for servicing and stabling purposes, located at St Philip's Marsh. A limited view of the depot area can be achieved following a fifteen-minute walk from Temple Meads. On 12 October 2013, No. 143618 is seen stabled in the depot yard.

On 3 January 2014, it is the turn of both No. 150128 and No. 158954 to be stabled here between duties. I can recall that, around fifty years ago, there was a number of withdrawn Warship class diesel hydraulics standing in a line here.

Bristol is a railway gateway for services to the South West with regular passenger services to Plymouth and Penzance via Taunton and Exeter. On a wet day in June 2019, power car No. 43162 is on the rear of a HST set leaving Bridgwater on a service from Cardiff Central to Taunton.

The seaside resort of Weston-super-Mare is served by a loop from the main line from Bristol to Taunton. The single branch line loop rejoins the main line at Uphill – around 2 miles south of the town. In the 1970s, loco-hauled passenger services to the west were commonplace, particularly during the summer holidays. On 20 July 1976, No. 46006 passes the junction on one such southbound summer holiday service.

The FOSS rover ticket area extends as far south as Tiverton Parkway station. This parkway station was opened in 1986 on the site of the former Sampford Peverell station, which had closed a quarter of a century earlier. On 14 July 2015, Cross County Voyager No. 220026 calls at Tiverton Parkway on a service to Plymouth. The town of Tiverton itself is just under 10 miles from Parkway station.

Bath Spa, Swindon and Trowbridge

GWR services between Cardiff Central and Portsmouth Harbour are routed via Bath Spa. On 16 July 2015, No. 158956 calls at Bath on a service to Cardiff.

Shortly after the departure of this unit, Freightliner's Class 70 loco, No. 70002, also headed west. It was on a light engine move to Stoke Gifford Yard in Bristol.

Further east, the Great Western Main Line's limit on this rover ticket is at Swindon. On 18 November 2015, London Paddington services were still in the hands of HSTs. Power car No. 43042 leads a service from Bristol Temple Meads as it approaches Swindon station.

This London Paddington service had power car No. 43171 on the rear. With effect from the end of 2019, all London services have been in the hands of Hitachi Class 800 series units. At the time of writing, however, both of these particular power cars have been retained by GWR for use on secondary services further west.

Melksham is one of the Wiltshire towns to benefit from much improved passenger services across the county in the last few years. On 15 March 2020, No. 166208 approaches the single platform station on a Sunday service.

The Wiltshire county town of Trowbridge enjoys a wider choice of services as it is situated in a triangle of lines serving Westbury to the south, Bath to the north-west and Swindon to the north-east. On 15 March 2020, a pair of GWR Class 158 units, with No. 158763 leading No. 158745, are calling.

Most of these Wiltshire services are now operated by GWR Turbo units displaced from services along the Thames Valley. On the same day, three-car Turbo unit No. 166215 approaches the station.

Heading in the opposite direction, two-car Turbo No. 165120 is slowing to make the Trowbridge station call in this view from the station's footbridge.

Around Westbury

The town of Westbury offers a great deal to today's rail enthusiast. The station enjoys a variety of passenger services as it is strategically positioned at a crossroads of lines, offering travel to the four main points of the compass. On 25 May 2014, No. 158954 calls on a service from Portsmouth Harbour to Cardiff Central.

At that time, most local services were in the hands of Class 150 diesel units, with No. 150249 seen here stabled in the diesel unit sidings between duties on the same day.

By the time this photo was taken on 15 July 2014 the first production batch of fifty of these units were thirty years old. Two-car unit No. 150108 is seen working on to Westbury Yard that evening. It will stable there in order to form an early morning departure the next day.

As already mentioned, the majority of passenger services in the county of Wiltshire are now in the hands of Class 165 and Class 166 Turbo units. On 16 March 2020, No. 165137 arrives at Westbury leading a five-car formation on a Cardiff to Portsmouth service.

Later the same day, No. 166215 heads in the opposite direction with a similar five-car formation bound for Cardiff. The unit still sports the earlier First Great Western livery.

GWR long-distance services to and from London Paddington are now in the hands of Hitachi Class 800 series units. On 16 March 2020, No. 800015 waits for departure on a service for Plymouth. Services between London and the West Country that are not scheduled to call at Westbury do not pass through, but use the station avoiding lines instead.

As well as this mix of passenger services, Westbury has long been an important rail hub for freight traffic, with the yards around the station area used for stabling locos and wagons from most of the main freight operators. On a Sunday afternoon, the yards are home to DB Schenker No. 66069, with Freightliner's No. 66615 stabled adjacent to it.

On the opposite side of the main running lines, No. 66514 is also stabled on the same day. Sister Freightliner Class 66 loco No. 66543 is just visible behind.

The following day, No. 70803 is seen arriving on a light engine move from Eastleigh. It will shortly reverse onto its rake of wagons and leave on a working to Stud Farm Quarry in Leicestershire for loading. Sister Colas Rail loco No. 70809 is on the extreme right with the diesel unit holding sidings in the centre.

The arrival of No. 70803 is followed almost immediately by that of Freightliner's No. 66955. After laying over in the yard to enable the Class 70 to depart, it is seen passing the station platform on a rake of hoppers from Avonmouth to Wootton Bassett Junction.

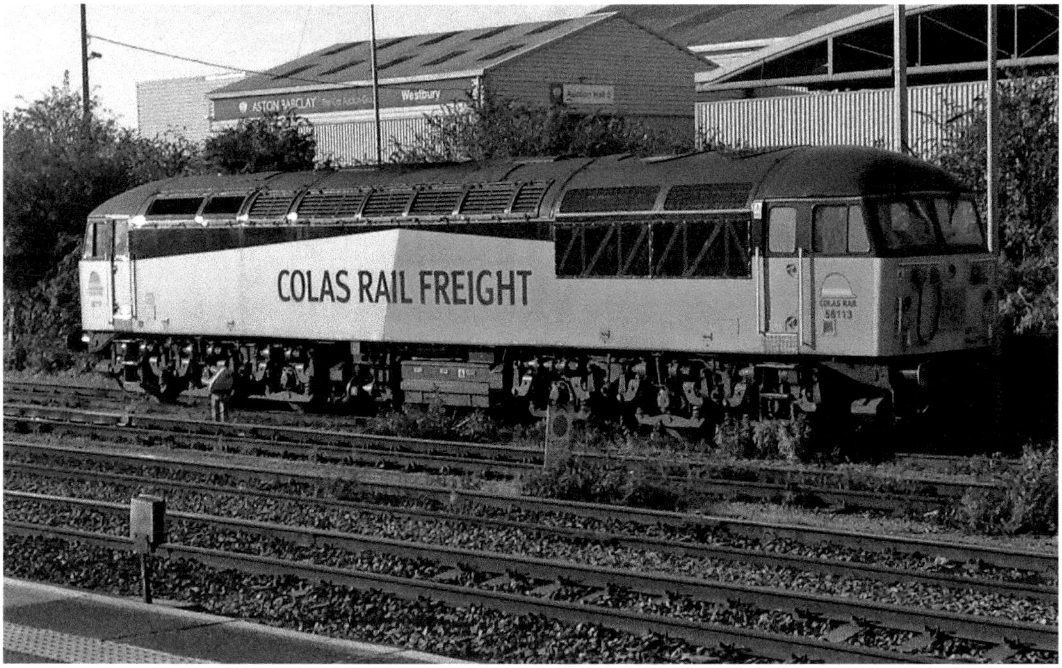

Colas Rail Class 56 locos are also regular visitors to Westbury. On 21 November 2013, No. 56113 reverses onto the yard, having arrived on a light engine move from Eastleigh.

Westbury is close to the Mendip quarries of both Whatley and Merehead. The small fleet of Class 59 locos have been associated with this stone traffic since the first examples were delivered in the mid-1980s. On 31 May 2012, No. 59002 *Alan J Day* passes through the station on a typical rake of stone hoppers. These Mendip quarries are an important source of hard stone for use in London and the south-east.

On 25 May 2014 it is the turn of No. 59101 *Village of Whatley* to arrive at Westbury. It has arrived on another light engine move onto Westbury Yard, this time from the quarry at Merehead.

Network Rail's high-output ballast cleaner (HOBC) trains are often seen in the Westbury area. On 15 July 2014, Freightliner's No. 66619 passes through the station on a rake that has originated at Fairwater Yard in Taunton.

There are a number of railway lines in the area around the town of Westbury, which means not all traffic passes through the main Westbury station platforms. Traffic between the yards at Westbury and Eastleigh can be viewed at Dilton Marsh station on the outskirts of the town. On 16 March 2020, GB Railfreight's No. 66738 *Huddersfield Town* approaches on a working towards Eastleigh.

One of the author's favourite locations in the area is at Fairwood Junction, around a mile and a half from Westbury station. On 16 March 2020, a pair of Class 158 units, Nos 158765 and 158750, approach the junction on a working to Castle Cary.

In addition to these GWR workings, Fairwood Junction sees the passing of South Western Railways' services between Westbury and Yeovil. On the same day, No. 159106 passes the same spot with a service bound for Yeovil.

The following day, sister unit No. 159010 is seen at the junction sporting its new operator's South Western Railway livery. It is on a service from Yeovil to London Waterloo.

As already mentioned, the substantial freight traffic from both Whatley and Merehead quarries passes through the Westbury area. These services, together with the dedicated fleet of Class 59 locos, are now operated by Freightliner. This Freightliner rake of empty hoppers from Fareham to Whatley, with No. 59002 in charge, has been routed via Westbury station.

The lines on the right of the previous photo are the Westbury avoider lines. Sister loco No. 59201 is heading in the opposite direction and taking the avoider line on a Whatley Quarry to Dagenham loaded rake of stone wagons. The dust blowing off the contents can clearly be seen as the train passes the junction at speed.

The station avoider line is in use again as No. 66570 heads through Fairwood Junction on a rake of stone empties returning from Banbury Road Sidings in Oxford to the terminal at Whatley.

In this final view of the junction, Freightliner's sister loco, No. 66955, heads towards Westbury on a light engine move from the quarry at Merehead.

Salisbury and Yeovil Junction

The city of Salisbury is served by both South Western Railway (SWR) and Great Western Railway (GWR). On 30 May 2015, GWR's No. 150120 is seen on a service to Great Malvern.

Salisbury is also served by the hourly GWR service between Cardiff Central and Portsmouth Harbour. On the same day, Springboard charity-liveried unit No. 158798 arrives at the station.

Sporting the more familiar GWR livery, sister unit No. 158951 passes the same point on a Portsmouth to Cardiff service. These workings are now in the hands of Turbo units operating in five-car formations.

SWR's diesel services between London Waterloo and Exeter are centred on Salisbury, with the Class 158 and Class 159 units receiving servicing and maintenance at the depot here. On 2 June 2017, three-car unit No. 159005 departs on a service to Yeovil Junction.

The South Western Railway servicing depot is situated alongside the station at Salisbury. On 24 May 2014, two-car No. 158880 is stabled in the depot's sidings between duties. These two-car units are often added to London Waterloo services prior to departure from Salisbury in order to strengthen trains as they call at the line's busier stations nearer to London.

Salisbury's station platforms see a limited number of regular freight movements. On 30 May 2015, Freightliner's No. 66590 passes through the station on a light engine move from its terminal at Cardiff Wentloog to Freightliner's base at Southampton Maritime.

On 14 July 2014, No. 66619 *Derek W. Johnson MBE* makes an appearance at Salisbury operating the high-output ballast cleaner (HOBC) from Fairwater Yard, near Taunton. Today's destination for the HOBC rake is a site near Grateley, between here and Andover.

Further west, the town of Yeovil is served by two stations, Yeovil Pen Mill and Yeovil Junction. Exeter services call at the latter. Yeovil's Junction station is in fact a couple of miles outside the town itself. On 2 June 2017, SWR unit No. 159106 is seen approaching Junction station – viewed from the station footbridge.

On the same day, sister unit No. 159103 waits to depart Yeovil Junction on a service from London Waterloo to Exeter St Davids. Westward from here, the FOSS rail rover ticket is valid as far as Axminster.

Heading in the opposite direction from Salisbury, services towards Eastleigh and Southampton serve the town of Romsey. On 5 August 2008, No. 150215 calls on a local service in the days when the franchise was operated under the First Great Western branding.

Eastleigh

The Hampshire town of Eastleigh owes its development to the railways of the past, being home to both an important railway workshop and depot for over a century. On 3 October 2015, No. 158880 calls at Eastleigh station on a local circular service between Romsey and Southampton Central.

A quarter of a century earlier and a number of Cross Country services were still in the hands of locos and coaching stock. On 31 August 1991, No. 47500 *Great Western* powers through the station on a service to Poole.

The freight working examples of the Class 47 locos were also common visitors to the Eastleigh area. On the same day in 1991, No. 47277 is seen on a local light engine move as it waits to move on to the main yard.

This Class 47 loco had just passed the locomotive stabling area alongside Eastleigh station. These holding sidings were home to a variety of locos that day. They included No. 33026 *Seafire* in the Civil Engineers Department livery of the time. The use of locos in this pool was restricted and they were generally only called upon for engineers' train operations at weekends.

The nearby works and depot areas are a few minutes' walk from Eastleigh station. That walk is generally rewarded on the basis of 'you never know what you'll see'. A view into the works yard on 30 August 2013 revealed an impressive line up, which included three Class 57 locomotives – namely, from left to right, Nos 57301, 57312 and 57305.

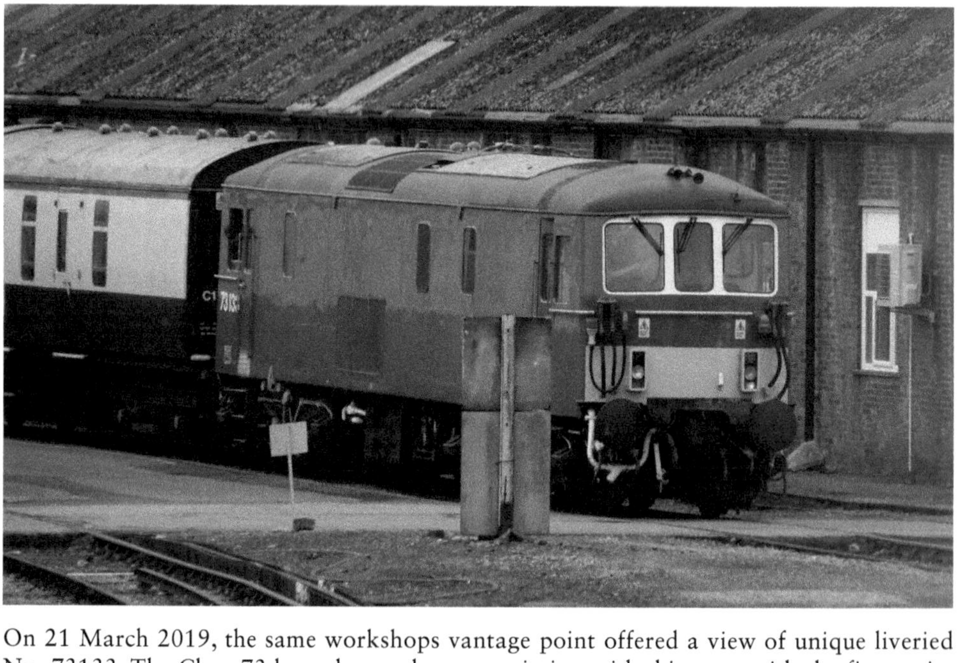

On 21 March 2019, the same workshops vantage point offered a view of unique liveried No. 73133. The Class 73 locos have a long association with this area, with the first series sub-class of these locomotives being built here in the early 1960s. This particular loco was built in 1966 and carried the name *The Bluebell Railway* for many years.

Class 37 locos also have a long association with the Eastleigh area, stretching back at least thirty years. On 5 October 1991, No. 37261 *Caithness* is working on to the stabling point adjacent to the station platform.

Almost thirty years later, on 20 March 2019, sister loco No. 37099 *Merl Evans 1947–2016* passes through the station platform on a Network Rail test train. This loco is currently owned by Colas Rail and dedicated to these Network Rail infrastructure duties.

Over the years the station at Eastleigh has rewarded the enthusiast with a wide variety of freight traffic and the assortment of locomotives used for haulage. On 31 August 1991, No. 60039 *Glastonbury Tor* pauses for a crew change in the station platform on a rake of short wheel base tank wagons.

A less common visitor to Eastleigh on 30 August 2013 came in the form of one of the few remaining Class 31 locomotives, No. 31190. It is seen arriving with a Railvac for delivery to the yard. This is another veteran machine having been built in May 1960.

There is a Travelodge conveniently situated across the road from the station entrance, with some of their rooms offering partial views of the station's rail movements. On 16 July 2018, No. 158880 is glimpsed leaving Platform 3 on a Romsey to Southampton circular working.

The same hotel window offers this view of No. 59103 *Village of Mells* on 13 July 2018. The freight train is passing round the back of the station on a rake of empty hoppers returning from Eastleigh to Merehead.

This hotel window view shows the main yard at Eastleigh on 15 July 2018, with DB Schenker locos in abundance. The locos on view in the yard include Nos 66037, 66955 (Freightliner), 66155, 66206, 66050 and 66183.

For many years a convoy of DB Schenker light engines, usually from Margam in South Wales, was scheduled to arrive at Eastleigh on a Saturday afternoon, in readiness for the weekend engineering requirements in the area. On 29 April 2017, No. 66034 leads sister machine Nos 66002, 66004 and 66093 as they arrive and prepare to reverse into the main yard.

GB Railfreight now has a significant presence in the Eastleigh area, including the use of the main yard here. The company's locos regularly stable in the sidings adjacent to the station. In this view, taken from the nearby road bridge, No. 73961 *Alison*, No. 73963 *Janice* and No. 59003 *Yeoman Highlander* were among the sidings' occupants on 16 July 2018.

The arrival of No. 50049 *Defiance* in GBRf colours was eagerly anticipated on the evening of 20 March 2019. It was released from the nearby works in the early evening and is about to leave on a circular light engine move to Romsey and back. It will then be joined by sister loco No. 50007 and leave for the London area.

Almost all passenger services in the immediate area are operated by South Western Railway and Cross Country Trains. There are also a limited number of Southern services that call here on South Coast services. On 29 April 2017, No. 377126 calls on one such service.

The nearby station at Chandlers Ford was reopened in 2003. The circular service between Romsey and Southampton calls at the single platform station here. On 30 April 2017, SWR's two-car unit, No. 158885, stops on an early evening service to Romsey.

Portsmouth and Southampton

The south-eastern limit of the Freedom of Severn and Solent rover ticket is at Portsmouth Harbour. On 3 October 2015, No. 158957 stands at the buffer stops at the terminus at Portsmouth's Harbour station. The unit will shortly return to Cardiff Central, an end-to-end journey that is possible using this rover ticket.

Southern operate Coastway passenger services between Brighton, Portsmouth and Southampton, including the use of veteran Class 313 units between Brighton and Portsmouth. On 24 May 2012, No. 313214 calls at Fratton on a Portsmouth-bound service. These units are some of the oldest on the network, dating back to the late 1970s.

The Southern fleet of Class 377 Electrostar units are used on these longer-distance South Coast services. On 24 May 2012, No. 377411 calls at Fareham on a Southampton Central to Brighton working.

Cross Country Trains' Voyagers operate limited stop services as far west as Bournemouth, usually from Manchester Piccadilly. On 14 July 2018, four-car No. 220001 passes Northam, on the outskirts of Southampton, on a service to Bournemouth.

Looking in the opposite direction from the same level crossing at Northam, No. 444028 passes on the rear of a westbound service from London Waterloo. The South Western Railway electric unit depot is to the left of this train.

Southampton Central is journey's end for Southern operated services along the south coast. On 16 July 2014, No. 377414 has just terminated at Central station and will shortly return eastwards towards Brighton.

On the same day, DB Schenker's No. 66046 is seen in the station platform at Southampton Central on an eastbound light engine move. It is awaiting the signal in order to follow the Southern unit through the town's tunnels towards Eastleigh.

Freightliner's main locomotive base in the Southampton area is the Maritime Maintenance depot, adjacent to the busy Freightliner Terminal. It is located a few minutes' walk from Redbridge station to the west of the city of Southampton. This general view of the depot area was taken on 30 April 2017. It shows a number of the company's locos stabled between duties, with No. 66957 in the centre foreground.

Freightliner usually have two Class 08 diesel shunters based at Southampton Maritime. On 14 July 2018, No. 08530 is stabled on the depot. Formerly numbered 'D3692' when new, this locomotive was built back in March 1959.

On the same day, a Saturday, No. 70007 was stabled on Maritime depot. The small fleet of Freightliner Class 70s are regular visitors between duties, often residing here throughout the weekend.

Sister loco No. 70019 is also stabled in the area, together with its rake of wagons, for the weekend when viewed on Sunday 30 April 2017. These sidings are to the west of the Maritime depot, close to Redbridge station.

Looking in the opposite direction, the extensive Freightliner Terminal itself can be viewed. In this general view on 15 July 2018 Class 66 loco No. 66508 stands in the foreground at the head of a typical rake of container flat wagons.

Around the New Forest

Several railway stations lie within this popular tourist area, offering some scenic railway views even if there's little variety in the rail traffic on offer when heading west beyond Southampton. The station at Ashurst New Forest is on the eastern edge of the area. On 30 April 2017, Cross County Voyager No. 220009 passes on a Bournemouth service.

The junction at Brockenhurst is the busiest station in the New Forest. On 14 July 2018, Voyager No. 221141 calls on a service to Bournemouth.

The same day sees No. 220021 heading in the opposite direction on a working from Bournemouth. Weekend engineering work further north meant it would terminate at Didcot Parkway, with a bus replacement service forward from there.

Brockenhurst is the junction station for the 5-mile branch line to Lymington Pier. For many years, these local passenger services were in the hands of two-car Class 158 diesel units. On 14 July 2014, No. 158885 waits in the branch line platform on a service to Lymington Pier.

By the time this photo was taken on 21 March 2019, Class 450 Desiro electric multiple units were employed on the branch's shuttle service. That day, unit No. 450564 was in charge of services. It is seen here approaching Lymington Town level crossing.

Lymington Pier station is the terminus of this single-track branch line. On 24 May 2012, No. 158885 is again in charge of branch line services as it waits to return to Brockenhurst.

A few years earlier on 31 July 2008, electric unit No. 421497 was in charge of the day's services. This was one of the last lines to see the use of 'slam door' electric units before they were phased out completely in 2009. Lymington Pier station offers a convenient connection with the ferry service to Yarmouth, Isle of Wight.

South Western Railway stopping trains also call at the New Forest village station at Sway. On 28 November 2017, the weather conditions were blamed for the late running of this local service from Weymouth to Brockenhurst operated by No. 450109.

On the same day, sister unit No. 450014 is seen heading in the opposite direction approaching Sway. It is on an empty stock working from London Waterloo to the SWR depot at Branksome.

New Milton station is situated just outside the south-eastern edge of the New Forest. On 21 March 2019, No. 444017 calls on a stopping service to London Waterloo.

Bournemouth to Weymouth

These Class 444 units, each with five carriages, are now the regular performers on most SWR services between London Waterloo, Bournemouth and Weymouth. On 30 April 2017, No. 444005 is seen on the rear of a ten-car rake leaving Christchurch on a service to London Waterloo.

The same day, sister unit No. 444040 is seen approaching the main station in the town of Bournemouth. A fleet of forty-five of these units was built by Siemens in Vienna. They were part of the programme to replace all life expired 'slam door' electric units, which did not meet modern health and safety requirements.

The impressive overall station roof at Bournemouth can be seen in this view of No. 444027 in the platform on 30 April 2017. It was damaged in the storm of 1987 and, eventually, Network Rail carried out extensive refurbishment around 2000.

West of Bournemouth these Class 444 units provide Wareham with two trains per hour operating between Weymouth and London Waterloo. On 22 March 2019, No. 444022 calls on a service to Bournemouth and onwards to Waterloo.

Later the same day new South Western Railway-liveried unit No. 444040 calls at Wool on a similar working. The fleet of Class 444 units are maintained at the company's depot at Northam.

In a look back to a familiar scene in the 1970s, Class 33 diesel loco No. 33108, fitted with push/pull equipment, works off the depot at Branksome with a pair of TR trailer units. This was the norm on London Waterloo services until the line through to Weymouth was electrified in 1988.

Further west, the town of Dorchester still boasts two railway stations. On 22 March 2019, No. 444026 leaves South station on a South Western Railway service.

Across the town on the same day, Great Western Railway's No. 166221 calls at Dorchester West on a service between Bristol, Westbury and Weymouth. Sadly, at the time of writing, the entire county of Dorset sees no regular scheduled freight traffic.

Journey's end for the London Waterloo service is the terminus at Weymouth. On 22 March 2019, No. 444036 is seen at the buffer stops. It will shortly return to London Waterloo.

GWR unit No. 165119 is also stabled in the platforms at Weymouth station on the same day. It will also retrace its steps and shortly form a service back to Bristol Temple Meads. This unit's route towards Westbury will diverge from that of the Class 444 on the Bournemouth and London line just south of the town of Dorchester.